Past and Present of
the Verbs to Read and to Write

Past and Present of the Verbs to Read and to Write

Essays on Literacy

———

Emilia Ferreiro

Translated by Mark Fried

A GROUNDWOOD BOOK

DOUGLAS & McINTYRE

TORONTO   VANCOUVER   BERKELEY

Groundwood Books / Douglas & McIntyre
720 Bathurst Street, Suite 500, Toronto, Ontario M5S 2R4

Distributed in the USA by Publishers Group West
1700 Fourth Street, Berkeley, CA 94710

We acknowledge for their financial support of our publishing program the Canada Council for the Arts, the Government of Canada through the Book Publishing Industry Development Program (BPIDP), the Ontario Arts Council and the Government of Ontario through the Ontario Media Development Corporation's Ontario Book Initiative.

ONTARIO ARTS COUNCIL
CONSEIL DES ARTS DE L'ONTARIO

National Library of Canada Cataloging in Publication
Ferreiro, Emilia
Past and present of the verbs to read and to write: essays on literacy / by Emilia Ferreiro; translated by Mark Fried.
Translated from Spanish.
ISBN 0-88899-556-3
1. Literacy. 2. Literacy–Political aspects. I. Fried, Mark II. Title.
LC149.F47 2003   379.2'4   C2003-903266-3

Design by Michael Solomon
Printed and bound in Canada

Contents

Introduction

I was first invited to address a publishers' convention in Mexico in November of 1997. It was the Second Inter-American Congress of Publishers, inaugurated brilliantly by Carlos Fuentes. My talk was so well received that representatives of the Argentine chapter (Cámara Argentina del Libro) asked me, more or less on the spot, to take part in the 26th quadrennial congress of the International Publishers Union, to be held in Buenos Aires in May of 2000.

That world congress began with profound words of reflection from Roger Chartier, but was soon swamped by presentations on new publishing and book technologies (Microsoft's "e-book" and MIT's "e-ink").[1] When my turn came to speak, at the closing session, I had the feeling that no one was quite up to listening to the sort of speech I had prepared during several weeks of contemplation. I was rather surprised at the rapt attention the audience gave me, and more so at the long, loud standing ovation the pub-

1. On May 13, 2000, Roger Chartier himself published in *Le Monde* an excellent report on the congress, calling it a "well-orchestrated drama in three acts."

lishers offered at the end.[2] This speaks better of publishers than of my presentation. After two days of practically uninterrupted chatter about international business and state-of-the-art technology, they found comfort in being reminded of the human side of their trade, that it exists in the context of a world profoundly scarred by growing inequalities.

These two talks appear together here with illustrations shown during the presentations. Commentaries on the slides of texts drawn by children were written especially for this publication.

This book includes another presentation, the keynote address of the World Congress of the International Reading Association in Buenos Aires in 1994, where I was given the association's International Citation of Merit. On that occasion I sought to reframe the subject of diversity, and was successful enough that it was later translated into Italian and French (two languages absent from that congress).

I would like to thank Enrique Tandeter for the opportunity to publish in one volume these three texts, which in my opinion share two characteristics. First, the pace of invitations to congresses, symposia and meetings of all types often means I have insufficient time for thinking about what I'm going to say, and frankly not all my presentations are well prepared – these three are. Second, all three articles are intended to awaken minds that have gone to sleep. They seek to explore rigorously and unflinchingly certain issues of direct concern to the broad spectrum of professions dealing with the existence of written lan-

2. A delegate from the United States later told me that if this had been a concert, I would have had to give an encore.

guage (from those who produce books to those who teach reading, by way of many others in between). To address such issues concisely but seriously has implications for both ideology and policy (publishing policy, policy on access to books, policies on teaching reading and writing, etc.). The conclusions I draw are neither simplistic nor schematic, and I hope they will open the door to action based on reflection and to reflection predisposed to action.

Emilia Ferreiro
Mexico, November 2000

Reading and Writing
in a Changing World[3]

There was a time, several centuries ago, when reading and writing were activities of professionals. Those who practiced them had learned a trade. In all the societies that gave rise to the four or five original systems of writing (China, Sumeria, Egypt, Meso-America and, very likely, also the Indus valley), there were scribes who formed a group of specialists in a particular art: to record in clay or in stone, to paint on silk, bamboo tablets, papyrus or walls, those mysterious signs so closely linked to the wielding of power. In fact, the functions were so differentiated that those who controlled what speech could be written were not those who did the writing, and quite often did not read. Those who wrote were not authorized readers, and the authorized readers were not scribes.

Back in those days nobody failed school. Those who were to take up the trade of writing underwent a

3. Plenary presentation given at the 26th Congress of the International Publishers Union, Buenos Aires, May 1-3, 2000. English translation (without illustrations): "Reading and Writing in a Changing World," in *Publishing Research Quarterly*, 16, 3, 2000, pp. 53-61.

rigorous training program. Certainly some of them failed, but the very notion of failing school didn't exist, even if there were schools for scribes. But having schools was not enough for the idea of "failing school" to take hold. Let's look at a contemporary parallel: we have music schools, and in them both good and bad students. If someone turns out not to have talent for music, society is not shaken, nor do psycho-educators worry about finding some peculiar sort of "musical dyslexia." To be a musician is a profession and those who wish to pursue music go through a rigorous training program. And, apparently, music schools everywhere are doing quite well.

All the problems with literacy began when it was decided that writing was not a profession but an obligation, and that reading was not a sign of wisdom but a sign of citizenship.

Of course, many things happened between one epoch and another, many bloody revolutions were necessary in Europe to construct the notions of sovereign people and representative democracy. The first texts made of clay or papyrus suffered multiple transformations before they became reproducible, transportable, easy-to-consult books written in the new languages that evolved from imperial, hegemonic Latin.

Readers multiplied, written texts became diversified, new ways of writing and new ways of reading appeared. The verbs "to read" and "to write" no longer had immutable definitions: they did not designate (and do not designate today) homogeneous activities. To read and to write are social constructs. Every epoch and every historical circumstance give new meaning to these verbs.

However, the democratization of reading and writing was accompanied by a radical incapacity to make it truly pay off: we created obligatory public schooling, precisely to give access to the undeniable knowledge contained in libraries, in order to build citizens aware of their rights and obligations, but schools have not managed to break free of the ancient tradition: they continue to teach a technique.

From its origins, the learning of reading and writing has been considered the acquisition of a technique: the technique of drawing letters, on the one hand, and the technique of properly converting text into speech, on the other. Only after having mastered these skills do expressive reading (the result of comprehension) and effective writing (the result of using the technique to achieve the producer's intent) appear, and it's as if by magic. Except that this magical leap from technique to art has been taken by very few students in those places where schools are most needed – and this is due to the absence of a historical tradition of "literate culture."

Thus we have the notion of "school failure," which since the beginning was conceived not as a failure of teaching, but as a failure of learning. In other words, it is the student's fault. Those students who fail have been designated, according to the period and customs, either as "weak-spirited," "immature" or "dyslexic."[4] Such children have something pathological, something that keeps them from taking advantage of teaching, which in and of itself and due to the generosity of its intentions, remains free of all suspicion.

But school failure is, everywhere and massively so, a failure of initial literacy and it could hardly be

4. In the 1960s, dyslexia was considered "the disease of the century."

explained by individual pathology. Around 1970, studies on the sociology of education relocated the blame for failure to learn, placing it on family surroundings: instead of something intrinsic in the student there was a "cultural deficit." In fact, a certain "social pathology" (the combination of poverty and illiteracy) was held responsible for the initial deficit or handicap. It's true that poverty and illiteracy go together. Illiteracy is not distributed equally among countries, rather it is concentrated in geographic, juridical and social entities for which we no longer have a name.

Today we don't really know how to classify countries. Before, there were "developed" and "underdeveloped" countries, but the latter seemed a pejorative judgment and came to be replaced by a euphemism: "developing countries." But how many decades can a country be "developing" without ever developing? (In fact, many countries that before seemed to be "developing" today seem condemned to be "underdeveloping.") There was a time when countries were grouped into two regions: "First World" and "Third World," with a supposed "Second World" that no country adopted as an adequate label for itself. And now we have returned to pseudo-geographic coordinates: the "East" and "West" axes have disappeared, while "North" and "South" have taken their place (which causes undeniable difficulties in the strictly geographic realm, such as placing Australia in the North and Mexico in the South). I'll speak of "periphery" when referring to this South, which does exist.

We don't know how to classify countries, but we do know what poverty is. We know – and it is useless to hide it, because the World Bank knows it and admits it — that 80 percent of the world's population lives in areas of poverty. We know that this 80 percent exhibits all the indicators of problems for acquiring literacy: deep-seated and hereditary poverty, short life expectancy and high rates of infant mortality, malnutrition, multilingualism. (We know, of course, that this 80 percent is also heterogeneous, since the inequalities between countries are equally expressed in domestic inequalities that are as or more pronounced.)

Despite hundreds of promising statements of national and international commitment, humanity enters the twenty-first century with approximately one billion illiterate people (while in 1980 there were only 800 million). Poor countries have not overcome illiteracy, while rich countries have discovered "functional illiteracy." What is this phenomenon which in 1980 put France on such a state of alert that it mobilized the army in the struggle against *"illetrisme"*? "Functional illiteracy" is the new name for a very simple fact: universal primary education is no guarantee that people will read every day, will get a taste for reading or much less take pleasure in it. In other words, there are countries that have illiterate people because they don't provide a minimum of basic schooling to all inhabitants, and countries that have functional illiterates because, despite guaranteeing that minimum of schooling, they haven't produced readers in the full sense of the word.

The period of mandatory schooling grows ever longer, but the results in "reading and writing" continue to give rise to polemic debates. Each level of the education system blames the preceding one for sending them students who "don't know how to read and write," and not a few universities hold remedial "reading and writing workshops." The fact is, not even schooling that goes from the age of four to well into the twenties (not to mention doctorates and post-doctorates) creates readers in the full sense of the word.

To be sufficiently "literate" to move along the school track is no guarantee of being literate for daily life. The better European surveys carefully distinguish between such parameters as literate for the street, literate for the newspaper, literate for non-fiction books, literate for literature (classic or contemporary), etc. To this list we must now add literate for computers and the Internet.

That is an acknowledgment that school literacy and the literacy required for daily life — for progressively automated work and for making use of free time – are not the same thing. And this is serious. Because if school doesn't teach literacy for life and work, for what and for whom is it taught?

The working world is more and more computerized, while school (our free, mandatory public system, that great democratic utopia of the nineteenth century) in peripheral countries is more and more impoverished, out-of-date and staffed with teachers who are poorly trained and even more poorly paid.

Actually, it's even worse: democracy, the form of government in which we all place our hopes, needs and demands, requires literate people. The full exercise of democracy is incompatible with an illiterate citizenry. Full democracy is impossible without levels of literacy above the minimum required to spell and sign your name. And we cannot continue betting on democracy without making the necessary effort to increase the number of readers (full readers, not decoders).

In the first decades of the twentieth century it seemed that "to understand simple instructions and be able to sign your name" could be considered sufficient. But at the end of the twentieth century and the beginning of the twenty-first, such considerations are untenable. Today social and work requirements are much more elevated and demanding. Surfers on the internet are boats adrift if they aren't able to make quick decisions or select information.

And schooling in peripheral countries, which have yet to learn how to teach literacy for the newspaper and library, now faces the challenge of the internet coming into the classroom, not because it makes pedagogical sense, but because "the Inter-American Development Bank and Starmedia Network established a partnership to bring the internet into every public school in Latin America and the Caribbean," according to newspaper accounts broadly publicized at the end of March 2000.[5]

Suspiciously, candidates of recent vintage for president or education minister in Mexico or Argentina have tended to run on the same slogan: "Internet in the schools," as if computers by themselves could be the trampoline for reaching levels of literacy never before attained, as if teachers — those out-dated and poorly paid teachers — could suddenly be recycled (or perhaps thrown away).

A few years ago I said in several fora, and I continue to maintain, that the new technologies will do education an enormous service if they help bury the

5. For example, in the business section of *El Financiero* of Mexico on March 29, 2000.

interminable debates on exhausted topics such as: Should cursive or printed letters be taught first? What should we do with left-handed students? Should we teach reading by words or by syllables? I welcome technology that does away with the notion of left-handed and right-handed. Now we write with both hands, on the keyboard. I welcome technology that allows us to separate or link characters at the writer's whim. I welcome technology that offers the learner complete texts right from the beginning.

But technology in and of itself will not simplify the cognitive difficulties of the process of learning to read and write (something that most pedagogical methods also ignore), nor will a "method versus technology" opposition allow us to overcome the misadventures of illiteracy.

Before returning to the unavoidable subject of new technologies, I'd like to delve further into the equation poverty ➞ illiteracy ➞ multilingualism. For decades we have heard expressions like "the struggle against illiteracy," a military approach that in Latin America also calls those who the school system rejects "deserters." The use of military language suggests an enemy to be defeated, and an elision from the abstract "illiteracy" to the concrete "illiterate individual" as the visible enemy is nearly inevitable, especially when the military image is associated with the medical image and we speak of "social pathology," "social disease" and the like, as if we were dealing with malaria or cholera.[6]

There can be no "struggle against illiteracy" (or against "functional illiteracy") rather actions intended to elevate the level of literacy of the population. We

6. All these expressions have been reiterated in official documents, national and international, from 1970 to today.

must understand literacy as a continuum from child-hood to adulthood, and within adulthood a continu-um of challenges every time we face a sort of text with which we have no previous experience.[7] Yet recently, and in the same military and militant spirit, the "International Day for the Eradication of Poverty" was proclaimed. I ask myself: What will happen to multilingualism? Will it also occur to them that it must be eradicated because it makes literacy more difficult and costly?

This is where publishers come on stage. You, the publishers, are the inheritors of a powerful and illus-trious tradition.[8] The lineage of publishers contains notable examples of all sorts: creators who never stopped giving new forms to our alphabet, endlessly inventing typographic characters (more legible, more elegant, better adapted to one or another kind of work). Artisans of the highest rank who made the book into a work of art. Families of publishers who passed sublime skill from father to son for over a century. Publishers who were also scholars and translators.[9]

You publishers have in your genealogical tree illus-trious defenders of freedom of expression, who from the very beginnings of the trade published texts that went well beyond the demands of the constituted authorities. I think, for example, of Étienne Dolet, a

---

7. For example, I teach at the postgraduate level, but I continue to make my students literate because it is the first time that they, as readers, come in contact with studies published in specialized journals and the first time that they, as writers, have to produce a peculiar kind of academic text called "a thesis."

8. To the Chinese, Korean, Japanese, Arab and Indian publishers present here, please forgive my ignorance, as I am only going to refer to the European tradition.

9. The overlap between the history of translators and the history of pub-lishers is enormously instructive.

printer from Lyon, accused three times of atheism and heresy and finally burned at the stake at the age of thirty-seven in Paris's Place Maubert in 1546. Étienne Dolet was a subversive of the time because he introduced France to works linked to the Reformation published in Geneva, but he was also a scholar, the author of an analogical Latin dictionary, of a treatise on translation and another on punctuation and accentuation. It is not known if the reason he was burned alive, along with his writings, was for being the publisher of those heretical books or the author of their prologues. But it is certainly true that 343 years went by before a monument in the very same Place Maubert acknowledged him as a humanist defender of freedom of thought.

Erudite and humanist as they may be, *publishers produce objects which are by nature incomplete*. A book is an object in search of a reader, and can't be realized as a cultural entity until it encounters a reader. *That reader is rather poorly characterized when defined simply as a client.* You can buy a collection of books to display them in your living room or office. Those books remain incomplete objects: *bibelots* without interpreters. A book becomes complete when it encounters an interpreting reader – and it becomes cultural patrimony when it encounters a community of interpreting readers.

That is why the work of publishers is unique: not only must they produce the most meticulously finished object possible, they must also be aware that that object, no matter how meticulously finished, will always be incomplete if it does not encounter "the others" who will make it complete. Those "others" are the readers.

Will the publishers of coming decades focus on producing books for 20 percent of the world's population? Will they return to the ancient tradition of elitist reading, contrary to the notion that literacy is required for democracy? Could we ask them — who could ask them? — to contribute to the completeness of their products, that is, to the production of readers?

The current situation is serious, but it is interesting because we live in a time of profound changes in the definition of the material nature of the object "book." Some proclaim to us a new democracy via internet while others are ready to organize premature funerals for the "book," that object with texture and odor, that "flesh and blood" which we grew accustomed to living with over the centuries.

On that topic, Roger Chartier warns us to make the effort to locate ourselves somewhere "between dreams of utopia and nostalgia for the past." It is easy, too easy, to praise the new electronic supports for the printed text; it is easy, almost banal, to apply the adjective "democratic" to a new technology. Let's look at an example that is emblematic. For decades eminent researchers maintained that the alphabetic system of writing was linked to democracy, because it is simple, perfect, scientific and easy to use. That belief was widespread. Yet three facts are enough to demolish this myth. First, in classical Greece, where the ancestor of the alphabet we use was invented, the number of free and literate adult males never surpassed 20 percent, as is demonstrated in detailed analyses by recent historians (Harris, 1989). Second, as a result of linguists' fascination with the alphabet, the native languages of America and Africa, no matter their structure, came to be written in an alphabetic system — a turn of events which did *not* bring with it universal literacy. Third, Japan, which has one of the most complex systems of writing, resisted all pressures to adopt the alphabet and has literacy rates higher than those of Europe or the United States.

Internet, electronic mail, web pages, hypertext... these are introducing profound and accelerated changes in the way we communicate and receive information. That is fascinating for any scholar of language and linguistic changes, but such instruments are not "democratic" in and of themselves (just as the alphabet is not democratic in and of itself). To struggle for the democratization of access to new technologies is one thing; to call them "democratic" is quite another. Those technologies demand, in contrast, capacities for more flexible use of written language than what we are accustomed to embracing. New styles of speaking and writing are being generated thanks to these media. To know how to surf the internet is already accepted as an educational objective or is well on the way of being accepted as one. Whether the malnourished and unemployed will learn to read and write in order to get onto the internet (while getting no school credits for it), or if they will be excluded once again, is something we don't know. Making predictions is a difficult and risky endeavor.

We speak of the future, and children are part of the future. No child needs to be motivated to learn. To learn is their trade. They can't stop learning because they can't stop growing. All objects (material or conceptual) to which adults give importance capture the attention of children. If they perceive that letters are important to adults (no matter why or for what purpose), they will try to appropriate them.

All surveys agree on a very simple fact: if a child has been in contact with readers before entering school he or she will learn to read and write more easily than those children who have not had contact with readers. What is this pre-school "knowledge"? Basically, a first immersion into "literate culture": listening to reading out loud, seeing writing, having the opportunity to draw intentional symbols, taking part in social events where reading and writing have meaning, being able to ask questions and obtain some sort of answer.

The relation between graphic markings and language is, at the beginning, a magical one that sets up a triad: an interpreter, a child and a set of marks. While doing this apparently banal act that we call "reading," the interpreter (who strictly speaking ought to be called "interpretator" for reasons impossible to develop here) informs the child that these markings have special powers: just by looking at them language is produced. What is it in these markings that causes the eye to make the mouth produce language? No doubt the language is peculiar, quite different from face-to-face communication. The reader does not look at the other, his audience, rather at the page. The reader seems to speak for the other there present, but what he says are not his own words, rather the words of an "other" who can multiply into many "others" that emerge from who knows where, hidden as well behind those marks. The reader is, in fact, an actor: he uses his voice so that the text can be re-presented (in the etymological sense of "presented again"). The reader speaks, but it is not he who speaks; the reader says, but what is said is not his own saying, rather that of ghosts who become real through his voice.

Reading is a grand theatrical event where we must discover who are the actors, the stage directors and the authors. (Without forgetting the translators because, to a large degree, reading is the presentation of another language, similar but different from daily speech.) Part of the magic lies in the fact that the same text (that is, the same words, in the same order) is re-presented again and again when given the same marks. What is it in those marks that allows not only the evoking of language, but the production of the *same* oral text, again and again? Children's fascination with reading and re-reading the same story has to do with this fundamental discovery: writing fixes language, controls it in such a way that the words don't disperse, or vanish or get changed around. *The same words, again and again.* A large part of the mystery lies in this possibility of repetition, reiteration, re-presentation (Ferreiro, 1996).

There are children who enter written language through magic (a cognitively challenging magic) and other children who enter written language through training in "basic abilities." In general, the first become readers; the others have an uncertain fate. Let me offer you two examples to illustrate what I mean. Two texts produced by intelligent children in the first years of primary school. Both still contain many spelling errors and problems with segmentation between words. But we won't focus on that, rather on the texts they have produced, texts that are perfectly legible despite the lack of punctuation (in both) and the utter absence of word segmentation (in the first).

Teresa is six years, two months old. Her school offers children positive experiences with written language every day. She has heard many stories read aloud (at home and in school) and she embraced enthusiastically the teacher's suggestion that she write a story that could be a little book. Teresa decided that she would write the story of a rainbow and she prepared the pages, drawing (with several colors) a rainbow on each page.

Standardized Version

THE RAINBOW

ONCE UPON A TIME THERE WERE TWO RAINBOWS
THEY NEVER COULD COME OUT OF THE SKY
UNTIL IT CAME

UNTIL ONE TIME IT STARTED
UNTIL ONE TIME IT STARTED TO RAIN

THEN THEY COULD COME OUT
BEFORE THEY CAME OUT THEY MET A PLANE
THE PLANE TOLD THEM
SOON YOU'LL ARRIVE

THEY ARRIVED IN THE CITY
THE SUN WAS SETTING
SUDDENLY THEY SET AND DISAPPEARED

AND THEY WERE IN THE SKY AGAIN
AND THEY WERE VERY HAPPY

THE END

1

2

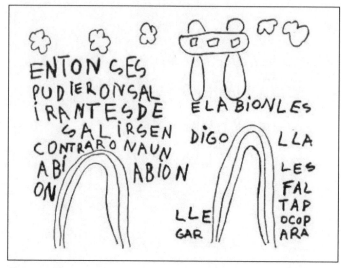

3

4

5

"The Rainbow," a story by a six-year-old urban girl who knows a lot about written language (despite writing in scriptio continua and with simplified spelling).
(Text produced in the classroom.)

Teresa is well aware that a story begins with one ritual formula ("Once upon a time") and ends with another ("and they were very happy. THE END"). She puts the story together as she writes and she stumbles a little in the first two pages ("So they never could come out of the sky until it came / until one time it started") but resolves it on the next page ("until one time it began to rain"). From that moment on the story acquires considerable narrative rhythm because Teresa demonstrates extraordinary knowledge of how to organize what she says so that it becomes "written language." In effect, the end of every fragment (as happens when read with natural intonation) is retaken to begin the next, but with a bit of elaboration. "Then **they came out. Before they came out** they met **a plane. The plane** told them: soon you'll **arrive. They arrived** in the city. (The placement of what is written in the two final pages has to do with the great rainbows drawn previously by her.) An undulating effect, forward and back, almost like waves in the sea. Teresa, at her young age, is already a promising writer.

Ramón is a rural child, from a small and isolated community. He has had no previous immersion in written language and his teacher is not willing to "waste time" reading out loud or coming up with challenging projects to get them excited about writing. His experience is limited to "free writing" and what he has lived first-hand. It is worth noting that it is hardly stimulating to find yourself faced with a blank sheet and have to write a "free text on chickens." But Ramón does his best.

texto libre sobre el pollo

El pollo es moy bonito pero come gesabos
y mois y pasto y los pollos comen
y se acen gordos y moy bonitos
y tanvien paben planguillos y tavien
el pollo se come y mor sabraca
que boano moli y le pohen tomate y chile
y cominos clabos y ou yos mes koene y lo
comen los ticos y tah vien los fritos
y tanvien tomas agoa

y asi se esa el texto libre sobre
el pollo

"Free writing on chickens". Text by a seven-year-old rural boy without previous experience with written culture. (Text produced in the classroom.)

Standardized Version

free writing on chickens

A chicken is very pretty
but it eats worms and corn and grass
and chickens eat
and they get fat
and very pretty
and they lay eggs too

and chicken is for eating too
and very tasty
good [with]* mole‡
and you add tomatoes and chiles and cumin cloves
and garlic
and it's really good
and rich people eat them
and you can fry them too

and they drink water too

and that's how you do free writing on
chickens

* added for readability
‡ mole is a sauce originally from Puebla, Mexico, made of chocolate and
several types of chiles

When you don't know what to write but you know
you have to fill a page, a list is a saving grace: "they eat
worms and corn and grass" / "you add tomatoes and
chiles and cumin cloves and garlic." Between those two
lists, an important transition has taken place: we've
gone from "chicken eats" (and "chickens eat") to

"chicken is eaten." Once the subject matter is turned into something to eat (and a meal for the rich), the text becomes a cooking recipe. And then, when we were expecting the piece to sink inexorably into the culinary world, Ramón rescues it with an inspired maneuver that transforms his entire text into a recipe (a recipe made of recipes) and brings it to a triumphal conclusion: "And that's how you do free writing on chicken."

Teresa writes in "written language," thanks to her considerable experience with books and reading; Ramón does what he can with his infrequent and not very stimulating classroom experience, focused on letters, syllables and isolated words.[10]

Who will have the will, the courage and the determination to break this vicious cycle?

In 1990, in Jomtien, Thailand, the goal of achieving basic education for all during the decade 1990-2000 was adopted. For the first time, the World Bank signed on alongside the international agencies UNESCO and UNICEF. Ten years went by and the results were disappointing. In April 2000, in Dakar, the World Education Forum met to allot another fifteen years to achieving that unfulfilled dream. And this will continue to be the case as long as the initial suppositions about literacy are not revised, as long as we continue relying on methods designed for training specialists and we ignore literate culture, which is the right of every child born in this epoch of interconnection.

My role as a researcher has been to show and prove

10. Both texts are by Mexican children. Ramón's came from a school run by CONAFE (National Council for the Promotion of Education), and Teresa's from a school advised by Myriam Nemirovsky.

that children *think* about writing, and that their thinking demonstrates interest, coherence, value and extraordinary educational potential. We've got to listen to them. We've got to be capable of listening to them from the very first written babbling — the moment they make their first drawings.

We cannot reduce children to a pair of eyes that see, a pair of ears that listen, a vocal mechanism that emits sounds and a hand that clumsily squeezes a pencil and moves it across a sheet of paper. Behind (or beyond) the eyes, ears, vocal chords and hand lies a person who thinks and attempts to incorporate into his or her own knowledge this marvelous medium of representing and recreating language which is writing, *all* writing.

The beginning of the millennium is a propitious moment for change, because there are many more of us who have something new to offer. None of us acting alone has the capacity to affect a phenomenon that has resisted all attempts to isolate its variables. But now we have new technologies for distributing texts, new insights based on detailed historical investigation into the ways writing is appropriated by different social actors at different historical moments. We have linguists prepared to rescue writing from the no-man's-land in which it was lost during the twentieth century. We have teachers ready to go beyond the futile battle over methods that ignore the person doing the learning. We have psychologists, psycho-pedagogues and psycholinguists with sufficiently valid theories for restoring our conception of the child as a thinking being in its existential totality.[11]

11. There are however psycholinguists who insist on reducing the debate to its most backward technical dimensions, utilizing of course new termi-

These curious boys and girls, keen to learn and understand, are everywhere, in the North and the South, at the center and in the periphery. Let's not infantilize them. From an early age, they pose questions of profound epistemological significance: What is it that writing represents? How does it represent it? By reducing children to technical apprentices, we belittle their intellect. By obstructing their contact with the objects through which writing takes place, and the many ways of "saying" when oral language turns into written language, we disparage their cognitive efforts, failing to acknowledge them or rendering them useless.

Literacy is neither a luxury nor an obligation: it is a right. A right of boys and girls who will become free men and women (at least that's what we want), citizens of a world in which linguistic and cultural differences will be considered a wealth and not a defect. Different languages and different systems of writing are part of our cultural patrimony. Cultural diversity is as important as biodiversity: if we destroy it, we will not be able to recreate it.

We come from an "imperfect past," where the words "reading" and "writing" were defined in changing, sometimes erratic, but consistently ineffective ways. We are headed for a complex future, one which those dazzled by technology call a "simple future," exaggeratedly simple.

Perhaps a convergence of efforts will be possible.

---

nology like "phonological awareness." Divisions of this sort aren't unusual, because they are inherent to all disciplines: not all historians think that it is interesting to focus on the way popular readers contribute to the meaning of writing in society; not all linguists consider that writing is a subject of interest for linguistics, etc.

Perhaps the incomplete objects produced by publishers will find budding readers (who are also producers of texts as well as producers of meaning). Perhaps primary school teachers and their students will renew their capacity for laughing, crying or being surprised when they read. Perhaps no one will fear the new technologies and no one will expect them to be the magic bullet. Perhaps we can entrust ourselves to future readers for the utopia of democracy to seem less unreachable.

Children — all children, I assure you — are willing to embark on the adventure of intelligent learning. They are sick of being treated as under-skilled or miniature adults. They are what they are and they have the right to be what they are: changing beings by nature, because to learn and to change is their way of being in the world.

Between the "imperfect past" and the "simple future" lies the seed of a "continuous present" that could lead to a complex future, replete with new ways of giving meaning — complete and democratic meaning — to the verbs "to read" and "to write." I hope that happens, even if the rules of conjugation don't allow it.

Past and Future of the Verb
"To Read"[12]

This presentation has one central objective: to analyze the future of reading based on understanding its past.

The verbs "to read" and "to write" do not have uncontested definitions. They are verbs that spring from social constructs, from socially defined activities. The relationship of men and women to the written word is not an unchanging given, and it has not always been the same; it was built over a long history. Reading will not mean the same thing in the twenty-first century as it did in the seventeenth.

Neither is the taxonomy of texts limited to an established group of genres. In fact, we are bearing witness to the appearance of new ways of speaking and new ways of writing, to new ways of listening to speech and new ways of reading writing.

We ought to situate ourselves somewhere between "conservative nostalgia and ingenuous utopia" (Chartier, 1997). At the nub of the debate is the question, How can we help create the new readers of the

12. Presentation given at the Second Inter-American Congress of Publishers, Mexico City, November 27, 1997.

twenty-first century, readers whom we ought to conceive of also as new producers of texts?

Are we facing a renewal (revolution?) of the definition of the text and the reader, of reading habits and ways of reading? I think the answer must be yes.

At times of radical change (and at the end of the millennium) it is fashionable to look at similar moments in the past, to try to discern what further changes may be in store — because even though such changes form part of our present, the present is always poorly understood because it gets swallowed by the pressures of daily life.

Let's look at some evidence of today's confusion, before we move on to interpretations:

a) The expression "computer literacy" conceals more than it reveals, because a generous proportion of the supposedly literate population of the planet turns out to be illiterate in relation to this new technology.

b) All of us here form part of an intermediate generation which lived through the birth of the computer. To witness the arrival of a technology or to be born when that technology is already established in society are two distinct situations. We are like those who witnessed the arrival of the telephone (from the sole receiver, wired to a predetermined location, to the wireless phone and the cell phone, the telephone has always been a status symbol as well as a tool for communication), similar to the generation that witnessed the arrival of recorded sound (from vinyl records to cassettes and compact discs…). Besides having access to the technology, having been born with that technology already established in society is an important factor. Owning or not a compact disc player, the mere fact of knowing that such a thing exists, modifies in fundamental ways our expectations and attitudes. Children in primary school today were born with computers as part of society (not in their homes, not in their schools, but in society). They are children who, because of that simple fact, are radically different from their teachers (nearly all of whom are infected with the virus of computer illiteracy).

c) As befits the spirit of the end of the millennium, we also hear proclaimed the end of libraries, the end of books and the end of authors' royalties. Critical thinking must have lost its edge, given that McLuhan's dictum ("the medium is the message") is cited with increasing insistence, while at the same time authors are offered peculiar contracts for rights to all or parts of their work, in any medium known or unknown, as if the message were still independent of the medium.

d) Everyone extols education as the key to belonging to the twenty-first century, but practically no one dares to acknowledge the new challenges facing literacy. Universal literacy remains an unfulfilled promise — despite massive efforts which hardly manage to provide textbooks (free or not) — yet no one dares to address openly the degree of illiteracy among teachers and their students, their incapacity to move from book (singular) to books (plural), not to mention from there on to computer networks and other assorted marvels.

It is not true that the first great revolution in reading behavior resulted from a technological invention. The first great revolution in the process of reading came before the printing press. Thanks to recent historical research, we now know that many of the virtues for decades attributed to the printing press began in the medieval period. The printing press disseminated changes that had been introduced in the seventeenth century by certain scribes; not the copiers in the great centers of medieval culture, but the Irish copiers on the geographic frontiers of medieval Christianity, who began to divide texts systematically into graphic units ("graphic words"). A text divided in that way allowed for nearly immediate comprehension, without the intermediary of the voice. That innovation took several centuries to achieve general acceptance, but it arrived in time for the great scholastic renewal of the eleventh to the thirteenth centuries in Europe (Saenger, 1997a).

Unconventional quick-copying procedures were invented to meet the demand for texts in the new universities (such as the *peciae* system, for example, used by professional copiers at the University of Paris since the thirteenth century). But of course it was the printing press that allowed the unfulfilled medieval dream to come true: to hold an exact copy of a given text.

Let us imagine the scene: this page of an ancient classic (illustration 1) was a challenge to the reader's capacity for interpretation. The page does not distinguish words and has no punctuation: both of these were left up to the reader. To learn how to "give voice to the text," to make it "sound," was akin to how readers of music notation today prepare themselves. Texts written during the classical period were made to be "spoken out loud" just like a sheet of music. And, also like music, the letters were the least of it (many of which had to be reconstructed given the abundance of abbreviations). What really counted was the interpretation. And then came social control over interpreta-

1. Text in scriptio continua (fifth-century copy of Virgil's *Aeneid*).

LIBER VNVS. 17

nihil fortuito effe factum,quoniam diuinæ ra
tionis difpofitio perpetua feruatur. Verũ aliâs
refellemus Epicurum, nunc de prouidentia vt
cœpimus,difleramus.

IN CAPVT SEXTVM.

Quod malum vanitatis . Sic habebat & Aldina
æditio,fed mêdofe.Ex vetufto codice reftitui,quæ
malum vanitas. Malũ enim hic interiectionis vim
obtinet:Vt in illo Terêtiano,qui malum alij. Hoc
non aduertens lector,mutauit fcripturam.
Nõ minus ineptũ effe videatur.Sermo videtur im
perfectus,nifi addas,q̃ dicere,aut fimile quippiam.
   De dei prouidentia circa vniuerfalem ho
      minis fabricam.   Cap.VII.

Eus igitur folidamêta corporis,quæ of=
fa dicũtur, nodata & adiuncta inuicem
neruis alligauit atcɜ conftrinxit,quibus mens
fi excurrere aut refiftere velit,tãquam retina=
culis vteretur,& quidem nullo labore nullócɜ
conatu, fed vel minimo nutu totius corporis
molem temperaret ac flecteret. Hæc autê vi=
fceribus operuit, vt quenque locum decebat,
vt́que folida offa cõclufa tegerent.Item vifce
ribus ipfis venas admifcuit quafi riuos per cor=
pus omne diuifos,per quas difcurrens humor
& fanguis, vniuerfa membra fuccis vitalibus
irrigaret,& ea vifcera formata in eum modũ
qui vnicuicɜ generi ac loco aptus fuit,fuperie=
cta pelle contexit.Quam vel fola pulchritudi
                                    c.j.

2. Text printed in Paris in 1529.

tion — a badly done reading would become equivalent to heresy a few centuries later.

The page from ancient classical times, like those from the beginning of the Middle Ages, is radically different from the page we have lived with for nearly ten centuries — one that suggests an interpretation (illustration 2) and allows the extraction of a fragment for citation (Illich, 1994). The changes that occurred in the "grammar of legibility" (Parkes, 1992) produced the sort of text that we find familiar: one with title and author clearly visible at the beginning, with numbered pages, with a table of contents, with divisions into chapters, sections and paragraphs, with a numeric or alphabetic ordering, with enlarged letters to indicate beginnings or titles, with punctuation that helps the reader find the external and internal limits of certain parts of the argumentative discourse. This sort of page gave rise to individual reading without social censorship. And this is the sort of page which is about to disappear thanks to new communications technologies.

Silent reading nourished two unforeseen consequences: heresy and eroticism. The new intimacy with the text set off two complementary movements in a single act of complicity: the freedom of the reader, whose interpretation was for the moment out of reach of censorship, and the freedom of the writer, owner of his pen and his unspoken voice, who could allow himself to express, in the intimacy of his cell or his bedroom, what no voice could express out loud (Saenger, 1997b).

The page inherited from the Middle Ages is today about to disappear. The page that allowed for systematic citation and for the very important distinction between commentary and citation (exact wording). The new technologies take this to the extreme. Unlimited fragmentation of a text can lead simultaneously to an excess of citation and unlimited potential for plagiarism, thanks to the superabundance of texts in circulation.

The medieval page made for a unique and private relationship between the reader and the text. The computer page destroys that intimacy. The illuminated and vertically positioned page on the computer transforms the act of reading into a public act.

In a short time we have gone from praising a "relaxed" physical approach to reading (abandoning the scholarly and schooled position in favor of reading lying on the floor, on pillows, in bed...) back to a rigid posture. The computer screen takes us all the way back to the epoch of the medieval *scriptorium*: hands in a fixed position on the keyboard, eyes looking at a text held vertically, back straight. Rigidity of posture and potential publicity of what is read or written are two bothersome consequences of the new technology.

Previous to the codex, readers' hands were trapped, holding up the ends of the scroll being read. Hands became progressively freer and we achieved that marvel of modern times: being able to take notes while reading. Now, in a certain sense, we are back to the scroll: scrolling through the pages we read or write on the screen has nothing in common with turning pages. The movement of the text is vertical, not horizontal, and our hands are trapped on the keyboard and the mouse.

Over time, books became progressively more differentiated and personalized. Their physical appearance allowed for immediate recognition. The computer, however, imposes a neutral image, in which all texts look alike. Let's take for example an e-mail message as opposed to a letter whose envelope has a material existence. When I look through my normal mail, I decide what to open and what to toss based on a number of indicators: the type and size of the envelope, the logo on it, the presence or absence of handwriting, etc. In contrast, emails don't allow me to take that first step and oblige me to embark upon a pseudo-democratic exercise. Every message has the same typeface, as if they were all worthy of our attention.

What I just wrote seems more akin to "conservative nostalgia" than to the real experience of users. But that's not the case. In an epoch in which we hear nothing but praise for new technologies, I think it wise to remind the publishers gathered here that what we are facing is a radical rupture with medieval practices — pre-printing press, if you like — and, in a certain sense, a return to some practices which we believed had been rendered obsolete.

Since the changes are quite rapid and research on the impact of new technologies has fallen far behind their evolution, all we can do is imagine which of all these changes will really have an impact on the acts of production and comprehension of texts, on the social uses of written language, and on education. Here is a list, intended more for reflection than as an agenda for discussion.

1) *The concentration of functions.* Functions that today seem linked were usually disassociated during past centuries: the author was not the material executor of visual marks; scribes were not authorized read-

ers; writing was for centuries exhibited to populations incapable of reading what was on display; monarchs had the power to control what could be written despite being illiterate themselves, etc.

For centuries the producer of texts to be written and the producer of handwritten works — the scribe — were disassociated. The work of the scribe was that of a slave or subordinate charged with the manual labor involved in writing. The scribe in the Middle Ages, for example, had to scrape and smooth animal skins and prepare the parchment; he had to make sure the goose feathers were cut properly with an instrument which even today we call a "penknife"; he had to prepare the inks, etc. (Ong, 1987). The author dictated but did not produce the handwritten work.

Technological developments permitted two functions which for centuries had been kept separate — the intellectual author and the material author of written works — to be unified. With that came the "author's manuscript," along with the notion of the author, which is a modern idea.

With the spread of typewriters, the "author's manuscript" was redefined. The intellectual and material author could now do without his own handwriting and could choose the typeface for production. To a certain degree, he started becoming a typographer.

With the arrival of word processors and the rapid improvement of personal printers, for the first time the material author and the intellectual author were united with the function of editor. This author can vary the size and font of the characters, determine the layout, insert drawings or boxes... and he can send his diskette directly to the printer. Camera-ready contracts establish a new author/editor relationship, whose fate I neither judge nor pre-judge. It simply seems to me to be a fact worth keeping in mind.

2) *The classification of texts is not circumscribed.* Not only do we have new styles of written communication, but also new ways of oral communication. Speaking to an answering machine spawns a new style of "speaking by telephone" which is different from what we knew before (and some linguists are beginning to pay attention to this). In the same way, to send a fax or an e-mail is not the equivalent of sending a telegram or, much less, of sending a letter. In analyzing these phenomena, the age of the users seems to be a crucial factor (in light of what we noted above regarding being around or not when the technology appeared).

3) *The distinction between image and text becomes problematic.* This distinction, extremely important ever since the introduction of "illuminations" in medieval texts, and firmly established in the Modern Era, is for the first time placed in doubt by new technologies — simply because the text can be treated as an image. The interface of text and image (and changes in the user's perceptions) is no doubt a subject worthy of greater attention, precisely because the new technologies arrived at a time of over-emphasis on graphic techniques to guide the reader's interpretation. (This, by the way, is one of the most obvious manifestations of lack of trust in readers. Particularly in scholastic texts, all sorts of techniques are used — drawings, charts or backgrounds of different colors, changes in typeface, etc. — because punctuation is no longer considered sufficient to guide interpretation by readers considered a priori to be incompetent.)

4) TV *screen vs. computer screen.* Before the prolifer-
ation of PC's we witnessed the spread of television
throughout society. Screen to screen, the two are similar — in fact, their interface is more and more dynam-
ic. But one came before the other, in terms of their
expansion across society, and there was a time when it
was thought that the image would replace the written
word. But computers strongly reestablished the primordial need for handling the alphabet efficiently.

The TV screen has something that the other screen
lacks: remote control. According to some, that instrument — not the screen — is the most innovative development because it has created a "culture of interrup-
tion and impatience" (Barbier Bouvet, 1993) that
leads to fragmentation of text. To juxtapose, to privi-
lege "strong moments" over transitions, to switch
continually without taking the time to analyze... These
are behaviors typical of the new generation (the one
born into life with television) which, apparently, are
most easily transferred to the other screen in contemporary life, that of the computer. We might suppose,
with some justification, that the way people behave in
front of these two screens could affect their approach
to printed material, not only regarding frequency of
use but also their manner of relating to printed material. "The habit of surfing among images (and not
only within an image) changes the way people roam
within text" (Barbier Bouvet, 1993). And, I would
add, it also changes the way people move among
texts.

5) *Linguistic imperialism and its orthographic consequences.* In principle, there is no limit to the capacity
of computers to process symbols. However, the fact
that technologies are developed in a language that

uses no accents or other diacritical marks leads, in practice, to the consideration that these are "unnecessary complications." Thus, different spellings, which along with different languages were considered during this century as equally valid "alternative ways" of speaking or writing, are now evaluated according to the paradigm of the "Latin of modern times," that is, English.

The French are asked to write without accents — which is equivalent to exercising unheard-of violence against that form of writing. In Spanish, the poor letter *ñ* suffers the strangest transformations: it is easily suppressed without affecting understanding in *niño* (child = nino), but that's not the case with other common words, such as *año* (year) which comes in my e-mail as *anio*, *anho*, or *agno*. The omission of accents (feasible in Spanish) will bring with it orthographic consequences, with or without the blessing of the Spanish Royal Academy.

Linguistic imperialism is expressed of course on other fronts: new words are adopted by assimilation, even when appropriate terms already exist in the language in question (*deletar* is now an accepted verb in Brazilian Portuguese, in place of *apagar*). Imperialism goes beyond the terrain of computers. The English word "literacy" has given way to aberrations like *literacie* (French) or *letramento* (Portuguese). We are all aware of the insufficiency of the Spanish term *alfabetización*, which leads to nonsense like *alfabetizado en una escritura no alfabética* ("alphabetized" in a non-alphabetic written language). But if *alfabetización* is anchored in "alphabet," using *letramento*, anchored in "letter," won't fix a thing. A better expression would be "literate culture," as it is closer to the original meaning of literacy (what with expressions like TV-literacy, today we often don't know which literacy we are speaking of).

All in all, in these modern times any proposal for "simplifying spelling" is inevitably tinged with orthographic imperialism.

6) *Generation gap*. I think all of us here have had the same experience: the only technical experts we can turn to for our problems with new technologies are young people. And the younger the better. When a "computer technician" over forty shows up at our office, we ask, Couldn't they send over someone younger? It is one of the few fields in which all of us who are over forty unquestionably acknowledge the competence of those who are younger. And that has undeniable implications for education.

And because we are also dealing here with education (specifically literacy, which is still the basis of basic education), the question is: Is the school, as a social institution, prepared to respond to the new requirements for literacy? The answer is absolutely not.

As we said before, these technological changes, which are probably redefining (like it or not) the terms "reading" and "writing," have occurred while universal literacy remains an unfulfilled promise. (According to UNESCO, more than 960 million are illiterate, two-thirds of them women. More than 100 million children, of whom 60 million are girls, have no access to basic education.) The oft-declared goal of "entering the twenty-first century without illiteracy" is unachievable. In percentage terms, there has been an overall decline in illiteracy, but in absolute terms there are ever more illiterate people in the world.

What's worse, the definition of "literate," on which these statistics are based, is obsolete. If we use as a definition, "to belong to literate culture" or "to be able to browse through the range of texts characteristic of literate culture, at least as consumers," the data would be shocking.

It is possible — and desirable — that technological advances will render obsolete age-old questions that even today crop up as valid topics for pedagogical debate: Should writing be first taught in cursive or block lettering? Should it be taught with a pencil or a pen? Is it the same for righties as for lefties? Such questions now have an immediate answer: The first step is to introduce children to the keyboard (be it that of a typewriter or a computer, which are basically the same). Writing in modern times is done with both hands and with separated characters.

Should children first be introduced to narrative texts and then, slowly, to other sorts of texts? Another quick answer: Browsing among several types of texts is the fundamental must-do of modern times. No texts come first, rather diversity is displayed simultaneously (just as with the acquisition of oral language). To learn to read critically and to develop selection criteria are not goals that can be postponed until the final years of primary school.

By what criteria should one text be judged better than another? The only answer that fits here is a question mark: It is possible that we are witness to a new textual aesthetic, a sort of "aesthetic of fragmentation," which I still don't understand, but which I accept as a possibility. The criteria for a "well-structured text" would have to change if we accept that we are in a moment of transition. Perhaps such changes will be more pronounced in creative literature than in argumentative academic texts.

In any case, if the new technologies manage to achieve a quiet burial for old and empty pedagogical debates, then bring them on. Because the pallbearers at that funeral will be the children who, interrogated by fringe researchers (myself included) in the 1980s, helped us move to a more complex understanding of literacy. These children, four to six years old, helped us to argue that reading was not equivalent to decodifying, that to be literate was not the same as "knowing the alphabet," that cognitive difficulties with understanding a particular way of representing language (writing) had nothing to do with difficulties acquiring one or another technology of writing. These children, four to six years old, obliged us researchers to assign new meaning to the relationship between writing and language, to apply *all* levels of linguistic analysis in order to understand reading behavior (rather than favoring just the phonological level).

We had to demonstrate that copiers are not producers of texts, to destroy the ritual of reciting syllabic families, to ridicule scholastic postures — and to allow the two great absentees from the traditional view to come on the big stage front and center where they belong: written language and the thinking child.

Those who did not understand what we were doing accused us of being anti-method. Others believed we were inventing a new method, but for reasons we wouldn't acknowledge we didn't want to give it its real name. What we were inventing were new questions, questions to which children gave such novel answers that all we had to do was amplify their voices to shake up drowsy educational thinking and yank it out of the moth-eaten closets of methodologi-cal debate. For example, the liberation of writing brought to light the existence of powerful writers who were only six or seven years old, as is demonstrated by this noteworthy piece by Samuel (six years, eight months). His story has a clear title and a convention-al beginning ("Once upon a time..."). Writing about castles and witches is not very original. The extraor-dinary part begins with his attempt to speak about a castle where "time went backwards," and to link that with actions in reverse order – "the witch first dried herself and then washed herself." The challenge that Samuel tries to take up, with his limited experience as a writer, is of grand proportions, and he doesn't seem to have taken good measure of his strengths, since the episode that follows breaks with the logic of the backwards world ("The witch cast a spell on a man and turned him into a toad and he hopped away."). But there is a saving moment, which both ends that false step and returns brilliantly to the original idea.

Standardized Version

THE HORROR STORY

ONCE UPON A TIME THERE WAS A WITCH'S
    CASTLE
TIME THERE WENT BACKWARDS
WHEN SHE WENT TO BATHE THE WITCH
FIRST DRIED HERSELF
AND THEN WASHED HERSELF
THE WITCH CAST A SPELL ON A MAN
AND TURNED HIM INTO A TOAD
AND HE HOPPED AWAY.

EL CUENTO DE TERROR
HABIA UNA VEZ UN
CASTILLO DE UNA BR-
UJA ALLY LAS HORAS
PASABAN AL REUES
CUANDO iBA A LABARSE
LA BRUJA PRIMERO SE
SECABA Y LUEGO SE LA
BABA LA BRUJA HECHi
ZO A UN SEÑOR Y LO
CONUiRTiO EN SAPO Y
SE FUE BRINCANDO.
Y AQUi ENPiESA LA
HiSTORiA PORQUE
DONDE LA ENPESE
ES ELFiNAL

Story written in the classroom by Samuel, six years, eight months old: "The Horror Story"

AND HERE THE STORY BEGINS
BECAUSE WHERE I BEGAN IS THE END

Exactly from that point on (the only in the entire piece) Samuel not only recovers his original intent, but also manages to convert the text into a "metatext" which refers to itself. In a flight of genius, which presages a great writing talent, Samuel ends his piece brilliantly: "And here the story begins because where I began is the END." (And, if that weren't enough, he makes the letters of the last word larger, giving the piece a graphic staging between the title, clearly differentiated from the rest of the text by a large space, and the END, placed in the center. Undoubtedly, to produce a piece like this requires extensive experience with stories and with readers, and a school context that is able to distinguish between constructing texts and following spelling conventions.[13]

Children of all times and cultures have known how to face the challenges of the culture they grew up in. Traditional schools, even today, offer them one definition of literacy, while society is beginning to demand another. That's the fate of today's children, born in a time of transition. Literate culture is not just literature or non-fiction books. Schools ought to provide access to the full range of books, but if they don't fulfill this function other spaces can be created or recreated: public libraries, cultural centers, television shows, movies, newspapers, computer networks.

That said, I'd like to state publicly my enormous distrust of the purely ideological proclamation of democracy via the Internet. It is like the oft-repeated

13. Thanks to Myriam Nemirovsky for access to this text, obtained in Mexico.

claim that the alphabet is the most democratic writing system of all (simple, scientific, easy to learn), and today we know that such a vision of the history of human writing is more ideological than scientific.

The real challenge is that of growing inequality, for the chasm that separates the illiterate from the literate has grown ever wider. Some have no newspapers, books or libraries, while others are flying with hypertext, e-mail and virtual pages of nonexistent books. Will we be capable of coming up with policies on access to books that can do something to reverse this growing inequality? Or will we let ourselves get carried away by the vortex of competitiveness and profitability, even though the very idea of participatory democracy perishes in the process?

Once upon a time there was a child, who was accompanied by an adult, and the adult had a book, and the adult read. And the child, fascinated, listened to how oral language became written language. Fascinated precisely with how something known turned into something unknown, which is the perfect place for taking up the challenge of knowing and growing.

Diversity and Literacy:
from Celebration to Awareness[14]

Literacy acquisition is no longer viewed as the simple transmission of a practical technique, carried out in a particular institution (school). Literacy is now the object of study by a plethora of disciplines: history, anthropology, psycho-linguistics, linguistics (beyond traditional ones, such as epigraphy, archeology, numismatics).

Many things have changed in recent years. I dare say that we are witnessing the appearance of a new multidisciplinary field. It is as if the subject of writing, abandoned in a "no-man's-land" by linguists in the twentieth century, had acquired citizenship in some country but we don't know which, in some territory but we don't know where.[15]

14. Inaugural address of the 15th World Congress of the International Reading Association (Buenos Aires, July 1994), during which Emilia Ferreiro was presented with the Association's International Citation of Merit. This article was first published by the Revista Latinoamericana de Lectura in *Lectura y Vida* (vol. 15, no. 3, pp. 5-14, 1994).
15. G. Sampson (1985, p. 11) cites axiomatic comments of L. Bloomfield's disciples, the first of which is, "Language is basically speech, and writing is of no theoretical interest." Bloomfield himself wrote, "Writing is not language, but merely a way of recording language by means of visible marks."

Something that seemed so simple — writing — has become considerably more complex. Now, besides the analysis and classification of the different systems of writing invented by humanity (an analysis with illustrious precursors which has also grown in complexity regarding the interpretation of the systems' evolution), we are sensitive to differences in the social significance of producing and using written markings, to the relationship between orality and writing, to the relationship between graphic production and textual authorship, to the conditions that give rise to distinct literary styles, and to the fact that pedagogical traditions acquire new meaning when inserted in a particular sociohistorical context.

Of all the topics that have come forward through these recent developments, I have decided to focus on one which, in my view, cuts across every level of analysis in which we might situate ourselves, and which I consider to be germane to this conference whose principal focus is "Sociocultural contexts for literacy." The topic is diversity, with its linguistic counterpart, translation.[16]

There is no way to avoid consideration of diversity when we study literacy, from any of its angles or facets: diversity of systems of writing invented by humanity; diversity of purposes and social uses; diversity of languages in contact; diversity regarding texts and the historical-cultural definition of readers, authorship and authority.

---

16. It won't be easy to speak of translation while I know I'm being translated. I expect I'll attempt a triple dialogue: direct, with the Spanish-speaking audience; indirect, with the translators; mediated, with the English-speaking audience. Rather than adding difficulties to the task, this will be appropriate for the subject at hand.

About the Conquerors and the Conquered

Conquerors and conquered have had to understand each other, in every place and in all epochs. The drama of the conquest of our America also had a linguistic dimension. Since those most in need of making themselves understood were the conquered, it was they who manifested a greater "ability at languages." (Always, in all epochs, the conquered, such as the Native American Indians, were considered infrahuman yet seemed quite skilled at languages.) In several accounts of this epic feat we find passages such as this one:

> the Indians seemed to have greater facility for learning Spanish or Portuguese than the Spaniards had for learning Amerindian languages. The first interpreters, for instance, were mostly Indians, and it is also known that Christopher Columbus captured several Indians and took them to Spain where they then served as interpreters — they were called "lenguas" ("tongues") or "trujamanes" ("dragomans"). (Pottier, 1983, p. 27)

Poor Columbus! Despite the fact that he came from a multilingual background,[17] he hoped that in these lands a single language would be spoken:

17. Analyzing Columbus's caravels as a plurilingual space is thrilling. It is said that Columbus himself spoke and wrote many languages, but all mingled together. On the ships they learned to speak, read and write in several languages all at once: Italian, Spanish, Catalan, Provençal, French, Portuguese. Were they really different languages, or rather the peculiar way Mediterranean sailors had of speaking? In other words, perhaps the Mediterranean must be seen as its own linguistic space, in contrast to the territorial (non-maritime) vision of the distribution of languages (See C. Blanche-Benveniste and A. Valli, 1997).

The procedure of first taking Indians captive so they would serve as interpreters was followed by Columbus on his four voyages...

But Columbus soon discovered that not all the Indians understood the interpreters, and that on these islands different languages were spoken.... On the coast of Central America he discovered that the new peoples each had their own language and that "they didn't understand each other any more than we understand people from Arabia".... All the expeditions proceeded in that way.... The Royal Orders of 1526, on the good treatment of Indians, authorized the capture of one or two people upon each discovery, and no more, for languages "and other things needed on such voyages." (Pottier, 1983, p. 99)

In *The Harp and the Shadow*, Alejo Carpentier depicts in memorable words Columbus's fear of finding a cross in the new lands (which would be proof of his failure, since he came in order to conquer in the name of the cross). But his linguistic fears were no less pressing. In fact, the conquistador had to confirm his rights over the conquered by means of a linguistic act of possession. If there were many languages to be translated in this act of possession/domination — and no one knew how many these "many languages" were — then the problem was devilish. Keep in mind that at the moment Cortés arrived in Mexico, more than eighty distinct languages and dialects are thought to have been spoken there; some calculations put the number as high as 124.

Between conquerors and conquered there were

many linguistic misunderstandings. Here is a single example:

> The Inca Garcilaso de la Vega recounts the following anecdote about an Indian named Felipillo: "He learned the language without anyone teaching him, just by listening to the Spaniards speak, and the unusual words he heard were the ones used by the greenhorn soldiers, I vote for such, I swear by such and others even worse.... This bold fellow was the first interpreter Peru ever had; and in his interpretation it is known that he did it poorly and contrary to the meaning, not because he maliciously intended to, but because he didn't understand what he was interpreting, and he said it like a parrot, and [regarding the mystery of the Holy Trinity] instead of saying, 'God is Triune and One,' he said, 'God three plus one makes four,' adding up the numbers to make himself understood." (Pottier, 1983, p. 27)

During all of history (ancient and modern) the role of the translator has been essential. Which is the same as saying that the role of contact between languages has been and remains essential. But because those in charge of translating have been subalterns, and because history is written by rulers, the importance of this fact has remained in the shadows.

Plurilingualism has been, and continues to be, the norm. Today most of humanity lives in plurilingual contexts:

> Multilingualism is a natural way of life for hun-

dreds of millions around the world. Although there are no official statistics, the fact that approximately 5,000 languages co-exist in less than 200 countries means that a great deal of contact among languages must occur. (Cristal, 1987, 1993 edition, p. 360)

At a recent UNESCO meeting, a colleague from Senegal maintained that "Multilingualism is what is most widely shared in Africa."

We know little about the linguistic development of children who grow up in plurilingual contexts, for a simple reason: most research takes place in countries that even today maintain the illusion of being mono-lingual.[18] People growing up in plurilingual contexts necessarily develop translating skills. Is that a met-alinguistic skill? No doubt it is, and despite the fact that linguistic awareness is in fashion, this skill has not been sufficiently studied.

On Scribes and Ancient Forms of Writing

The form of writing that gave birth to the alphabet arose in ancient Mesopotamia, within contexts that were multilingual and multicultural. We can't say that plurilingualism helped it along, but we can state that plurilingualism posed no impediment to its creation and its extraordinary spread. Composed of a mixture of logograms, phonetic (syllabic) signs and silent cate-

18. "One out of every seven residents of the United States speaks a foreign language at home, which signifies a marked increase compared to 1980.... The new census report shows that the 31,800,000 speakers of foreign languages use 329 different languages. The most common is Spanish, spoken by over 17 million (54 percent of those who don't speak English at home). That's ten times the number who speak French, which is the second language on the frequency list." (*Today*, United States, April 28, 1993)

gorical determinants, cuneiform writing expanded over an extensive region and was used to write various languages that were linguistically unrelated.

The territory where writing emerged at the end of the fourth millennium B.C.,[19] was occupied symbiotically by various ethnic groups, with two language groups predominating: Semites (which by convention we call "Akkadians"), who came from the northern edge of the great Syrian-Arab desert; and "Sumerians," whose language was radically different and who must have come from the southeast. The two initially separate groups quickly became intermingled. The Sumerians invented writing but were literally absorbed during the third century B.C. by their Akkadian neighbors. (Bottéro, 1990)

Invented by the Sumerians, cuneiform writing outlasted the language that spawned it. It was taken up by the Babylonians (nomad Semites who came from the Syrian desert). In the region of Elam (southeast Iran) it was used to write Akkadian and Elamite (a non-Semitic and non-Indo-European language). The Persians retained the Elamite language and writing, and turned them into administrative instruments. To the west, the people of Ur (who spoke a non-Semitic and non-Indo-European language) used the cuneiform system to write their language, and through them it reached the Hittites (Indo-Europeans), who used cuneiform writing not only for their own language but also for those of neighboring peoples.

Writing with the cuneiform system on clay tablets spread throughout Asia Minor, Syria and Anatolia.

19. "Today we can state that the proto-cuneiform system of writing was probably invented as a complete system at a particular time at the end of the fourth millennium before Christ in southern Iraq, in one of the cities of Sumeria, very likely in Uruk." (Michalowski, 1994, p. 54)

We still do not know the exact date when this writing disappeared. (The most recent cuneiform tablet with confirmed dating is from 75 A.D.) "That means the cuneiform system was utilized during three millennia and a half, approximately." (Michalowski, 1994, p. 63).

Thus, before the Greek alphabet emerged there were extensive efforts to translate and adapt a successful system of writing to a multiplicity of languages.[20]

Fortunately, current research is distancing us from the traditional telling of the history of writing as an inexorable march toward the alphabet, and is also distancing us from the traditional vision that the alphabetic system is the one that has all virtues and no defects, that by being simple, economical, precise, the alphabet will take us by the hand and carry us to universal literacy, rational thought, modern science and democracy.

Acknowledging the mixed nature of the forms of writing derived from the Greek alphabet (none of which is purely alphabetic) — like the study of distinct systems of writing in and of themselves (and not as simple preparatory stages leading to the alphabet)[21] and their intimate relation to the languages for which

20. For example, the logogram for sky was read "am" in Sumerian, "samu" in Akkadian and "nepis" in Hittite. The silent determinants fulfilled a primordial textual organizing function (determinants of names of masculine and feminine persons, gods, cities). The spread of the same determinants allowed for interpreting cuneiform texts written in unknown languages or dialects (for example, the deciphered tablets of Elba, in the north of Syria, written in an unknown language, a Semitic dialect of the northeast of which there is no other evidence). (Godart, 1992)

21. One of the great achievements of twentieth-century linguistics was to study each language in and of itself, instead of as compared to the prototype of a "perfect language" (Latin). What was needed was to do the same thing in the case of writings: to study each in and of itself, instead of as compared to the ideal of alphabetic writing.

they were created — will allow us to have a more balanced and objective vision of this history.

What is undeniable is that the alphabet was also invented thanks to contact among and differences between languages. In fact, the alphabet seems to have originated due to translation problems (with deforming assimilation). The Greeks could not possibly have already had the idea of alphabetic writing and only needed some arbitrary shapes in order to create it. That can't be the case because man had been creating graphic markings since the most remote antiquity. (Although it is equally clear that there is a vast difference between a group of graphic markings and a system of graphic shapes that can be interpreted linguistically.)

Most probably, the Greeks encountered a version of the Semitic alphabet used by the Phoenicians. No matter whether it was the Phoenicians or the Canaanites, the important point is that they not only had a group of shapes, but a group of shapes that was ordered (an "alphabetical order"), and acrophonic names for those shapes: words that began with the sounds corresponding to the letters so named. It is not hard to imagine the linguistic dialogue that might have taken place between Semitic language speakers, for whom meaning is linked to the consonant skeleton, and Greek speakers, for whom vowels are important for distinguishing meaning. The Phoenician alphabet had initials for sounds that didn't exist in Greek: pharyngeal sounds and glottal stops. The word that identified the first letter was "?alp" and in it Phoenicians heard an initial consonant, while the Greeks heard a vowel: thus, the first letter of the Greek alphabet is "alpha," a word without any meaning in Greek. (See Sampson, 1985, ch. 6)

The advantage of this interpretation of history is that it avoids all the difficulties inherent to the previous "official version," according to which (and thanks to the ineffable "Greek genius") the Greeks recognized the consonants of their own system and those of the Phoenician one, and immediately realized that representation of vowels was lacking.[22]

According to the new interpretations of that crucial historical moment in European history, a basic misunderstanding must have taken place when alphabetic writing was created: the typical misunderstanding that always occurs between speakers who don't share the same phonetic system. I don't recognize that sound, so I assimilate it into one of my own; your "?a" is my "a," that is, a particular way of saying "a" without the initial glottal phoneme. The alphabet emerged in a context of commercial (and linguistic) exchange.

Whether the Greek miracle arose from a deformed assimilation or not matters little, because the event had consequences known to us all. I only wish to highlight the fact that there were issues of translation (and interpretation) in the origin of our alphabet, because there were languages in contact with one another.

It was also thanks to translation that Egyptian writing was deciphered: the Rosetta Stone, which presented the same text written in two languages (Greek and Egyptian) and in three types of characters (hieroglyphic, demotic and Greek). The Rosetta Stone is also a testimony to the pluri-literacy that was common in

22. If they could have done that, the Greeks must have possessed a phonological awareness far superior to that of the illiterate adults of the twentieth century.

Egypt under the rule of the Greeks, where traditional writing had not been lost. The priests, in charge of the schools for scribes, introduced the invaders' writing without giving up their own. (In 332 B.C., Alexander the Great conquered Egypt and expelled the Persians, but the regime of the Pharaohs did not change. See Thompson, 1994, pp. 71-72.)

In ancient classical Mesopotamia and Egypt, the scribes worked with more than one language, and their training included the use of written languages without the oral counterpart. "The first systems of writing almost never used vernacular language for writing." (Michalowski, 1994, p. 59)

> Scribes throughout the Near East, including Indo-European Anatolia, Iran and Egypt, spoke fluent Akkadian and Sumerian, neither of which were their native language, and when they invented their own systems of writing, such as in Ugarit on the Mediterranean coast, they maintained their old cuneiform system. The same scribes wrote in two, three or more different languages and in different scripts. (Michalowski, 1994, p. 60)

Many of the virtues attributed to the characters themselves (script) or to the system (alphabetical) ought to correspond to the society that took charge of administering that script. The secularization of writing emerged as one basic factor. (For the first time, it seems, schools became independent of temples.)

If it is the case that the great Greek breakthrough was not the invention of the alphabet, but rather a wider distribution of control over speech that can be written — a step away from the professionalization of scribes — then the history of writing systems becomes linked to the history of literacy, and to the ways in which the use of written markings was controlled, employed and deployed, as well as to the ways in which control was exercised over what speech must or could be written. Let's not forget that scribes in ancient times wrote for other scribes, not for the authorities (who often could not read) nor for the people who attended "silent writing," a writing symbolic of authority, writing "to be seen, not read." (Detienne, 1986, cited by Michalowski, 1994)

The alphabet emerged in a context of linguistic exchange. It emerged in a context of shared differences. Soon the system stopped being purely alphabetical (differences in the length of vowels were no longer systematically transcribed). The recognition that all writing systems are mingled, that the alphabetic ideal is precisely that, an ideal never reached, is germane to the purpose of this article, because incompatibilities among differences arise from the belief held by one or all parties that each of them represents an ideal incompatible with other ideals.

Literacy and Schooling

Now let's take a leap to the present and the predictable future. (Though it would be quite worthwhile to delve into the thrilling subject of diglossia during the Middle Ages, when the Romance languages, *lengua illiterata*, manage to emerge within Latin, such that even Charlemagne wrote in Latin what he spoke in Romance language, and he spoke in Romance what he would then write in Latin, which is what lies at the root of the famous "mute letters" that would later impregnate French. (Blanche-Benveniste, 1993)

The history of literacy, precisely as we have been learning, is filled with multilingualism, with multiliteracy and cultural exchanges. The history of literacy in the context of obligatory schooling is another story.

Free and obligatory public schooling in the twentieth century is a legacy of the previous century, and was charged with an extremely important historic mission: to create a single people, a single nation, liquidating differences among citizens considered equals before the law. The primary trend was to buttress equality with homogeneity. If citizens were equal before the law, then school ought to help create equal citizens by homogenizing children, despite their initial differences. (School uniforms did their part in many places, by making visible that apparent homogeneity.)

Charged with the task of homogenizing, equalizing, the school could hardly appreciate differences. As part of its mission, the school struggled not only against differences in language, but also against differences in dialect, thus contributing to the myth that a single model dialect is needed to access written language.

The negation of differences was thus a central character of the first phase of the democratization of learning. The intent was to go extremely far in that negation, as became evident with the emergence of new nations, particularly those that had indigenous populations before the Conquest. At the dawn of the twentieth century there was an extraordinary polemic in Mexico regarding the Indian problem. The positivist Justo Sierra declared:

Our country's polyglossia is an obstacle to the propagation of culture and the inculcation of complete awareness of the fatherland, and only widespread obligatory schooling in the entire country could overcome such a dangerous barrier. (Brice-Heath, 1986, p. 124)

No place was foreseen for the conservation of indigenous languages. All Justo Sierra did was take up the discourse that had been on liberal politicians' lips since 1830 (progressives for their era): for the Mexican nation to be constituted, the Indians (three-fifths of the population at that time and, moreover, poor and landless) could not be considered or treated separately. José Ma. Mora proposed that instead of speaking of "Indians and non-Indians," we should speak of "poor and rich." By means of education (which presumed teaching literacy in Spanish) the Indians could take part like other citizens in the economic benefits of the nation. Mora proposed that the first constitutional congress uproot the word "Indian" from public and legal usage, and that the law declare: "*Indians no longer exist*" (Brice-Heath, 1986, p. 103). This was a remarkable example of negation of differences, motivated by reasons considered progressive at the time.

The negation of differences historically speaking could spring from progressive attitudes. In the same way, the recognition of differences could lead to segregationist attitudes and respond to anti-progressive interests. That is what happened in South Africa recently (Samuels, 1990). The specific needs of native South Africans were invoked in order to establish the apartheid system (Bantu Education Act of 1953). The commission in charge of laying the foundations of an educational system specifically for native South Africans (Native Education Commission) was asked to formulate "principles and purposes of education for natives as an independent race, education which should take into consideration their past and present, their inherent racial qualities, their distinctive characteristics and aptitudes, and their needs under ever-changing social conditions."

Therefore, recognition of differences has not always been linked to social justice, nor has their negation always been achieved by the negation of social justice. What I wish to emphasize is that right from the very beginning public schooling in new nations has, as an institution, experienced difficulties working with diversity.

Despite the efforts of scholastic institutions, differences subsist. The first differences to be clearly acknowledged were individual differences in school performance. But I'm not dealing here with individual differences, rather with those that affect social groupings, or more specifically with those that affect individual children who belong to such social groupings.[23]

In the specific field of literacy, the conversion of writing — social activity par excellence — into a school-bound activity helped accentuate the trend toward the negation of differences. Literacy was taught by a single method, with a single preferred (controlled and domesticated) sort of text, according to a single definition of reader, a single system of valid writing, and a fixed way of speaking.

---

23. It is well known that acknowledgement of such individual differences helped lead to both intelligence tests and special education schools, thus in no way changing the ideology of schooling. "Exceptional" children were transferred out of the school institution to other "special" institutions.

Public schools in Latin American countries, ever more overcrowded and less prepared technically, ever more impoverished in all senses, went from negating heterogeneity to acknowledging it as an unavoidable evil.

But the root of unavoidable differences was always found within the child himself (a deficit or pathology) or in something outside the school (lack of stimulus in the family setting). The school was never responsible for differences. The school struggled to eliminate them, without ever being able to compensate fully for social, family or individual deficits (including linguistic "deficits").

Only in recent years, and thanks to intensive research, have we learned again to link the concepts of diversity and literacy. We know that literacy is best acquired

a) when students are allowed to interpret and produce a diversity of texts (including the diverse purposes for which texts are created);

b) when students are provided with diverse sorts of interactive experiences with written language;

c) when students are challenged by a diversity of communicative purposes and functional situations linked to writing;

d) when the diversity of problems to be faced in producing a written message is acknowledged (problems with graphic representation, with spacial organization, with spelling of words, with punctuation, with lexical selection and organization, with textual organization, etc.);

e) when students are asked to work with texts from a diversity of viewpoints (author, proofreader, commentator, evaluator, actor, etc.); *and*

f) when, finally, it is presumed that the diversity of students' experiences enriches their interpretation of a text and helps them distinguish between the exact wording and the intended meaning; when the diversity of levels of conceptualization of writing allows for creating situations of exchange, justification and awareness-building that facilitate rather than hinder the process; when we presume that children think about writing — and not that all of them think the same thing at the same time.

Thinking about the relationship between speaking and writing implies a complex psychological operation of "objectification" of speech, in which writing itself plays a fundamental role. Children acquire oral language via situations of effective communication, as an instrument for social interaction. They know what linguistic communication is used for. But when they try to understand writing they must objectify speaking, that is, they must turn it into an object of reflection: to discover that it has parts that can be ordered, interchanged, classified; to discover that similarities and differences in signifiers are not parallel to similarities and differences in meaning; to discover that there are many ways of "saying the same thing" in speaking and writing; to construct a "metalanguage" for speaking about language, now converted into an object of thought. Differences in ways of speaking convey an immediate interest in thinking about language, because differences highlight issues that similarities hide.

The great linguist Roman Jakobson (1959) said, "Equivalence in difference is the cardinal problem of language and the pivotal concern of linguistics."

Comparative linguistic research could not have developed if languages weren't translatable. It is evident that only on rare occasions can translations be "word for word," and translation, as I pointed out at the beginning, engenders its own areas of incommunicableness, because linguistic differences are intimately linked to cultural differences. Misunderstandings exist alongside the potential for translation. It is the misunderstandings that interest me, because I think linguistic differences, in general, best exemplify similar cultural differences.

Linguistic differences — and cultural ones — ought not to be minimized. It is not enough to make speeches praising cultural diversity. Personally, I tend to do precisely that, especially when I hear ecologists praise the biological diversity of our planet (and the need to conserve it) while forgetting cultural diversity, which needs to be preserved just as much as biological diversity, because we will not be able to recreate it.

However, we need to recognize that linguistic (and cultural) diversity is also at risk of extinction. The supposedly "neutral" ideas called "modernization" and "globalization" carry with them a scorn for linguistic and cultural variations. (I say "linguistic and cultural" not to oppose these terms, rather to emphasize the role of language within culture.) We are witnessing the spread of globalization, but at the same time the rebirth of the most narrow of nationalisms. Great population migrations: people moving to the countries of the North in search of that world of abundance and wealth promoted on international television. Increase in population in the countries of the South. Growing unemployment in the most developed countries. This provides a favorable context for the appearance of a thousand forms of discrimination and racism. It is easy to be tolerant of "the other" when you live amid abundance. And very easy to fall prey to intolerance when "the other" (black or mulatto, woman or country hick, Hispanic or Indian) turns up and competes for your housing, jobs, and health and education services.

What is the mission of the public school in this context? It can no longer pretend to be the homogenizer, because other much more powerful forces are achieving that more quickly and efficiently than schools ever could. Transnational TV has managed to get children, youth and adults to all desire the same possessions, to aspire to the same lifestyle, to know the same things and be ignorant of the same other things, to have the same role models. It is a fact. I don't plan on making a typical antimedia speech lamenting the fact that the number of hours children spend in front of the television screen rivals and defeats the number of hours spent in front of teachers and a blackboard.

On the contrary, I believe that the way TV exists in today's world offers us a unique opportunity to *rethink* schooling, and to discover a new mission for it (perhaps just as unreal as the one it had during the last century, but equally necessary): that of helping all children on the planet to understand and appreciate the value of diversity.

In linguistic and cultural diversity, there is no risk, only richness, in that it *creates contexts for communication between differences and despite differences.* The risk lies in lack of communication among heterogeneous people. That is why we need translators. Several years ago in Geneva I interviewed a bilingual girl, the daughter of Spaniards, and I asked her if "*pato*" and "*canard*" were the same words or different ones. I recall her answer perfectly: "The words are the same, only they are pronounced differently." Here we have an original idea about translation, from the mouth of a five-year-old bilingual girl.

My intention is to warn against a common use of cultural differences that I would call "folkloric," which portrays it as a festive celebration of diversity. No. Understanding diversity requires a dramatic dimension. How is it possible for peoples who think that the past is right here with us, because we can see it, while the future lies behind because we cannot see it (as the Mayas think), to understand peoples who visualize the future topographically as ahead of us and the past as behind? Are we not aware that in Latin America, thousands of children preferred and still prefer to remain mute in school rather than admit publically that they speak a scorned Indian language? Are we not aware that today in Europe there are Moroccan and Turkish girls who are expelled from school because they refuse to pull back their traditional veils during class?[24]

In that same Europe that still recalls the horrors of the negation of differences experienced only fifty years ago, horrors that led to persecution and physical destruction in the name of purifying the race.

We must acknowledge the dramatic dimension, because we risk sliding from celebration to negation in the swing of a pendulum so common to the field of education.

Could I ask primary school teachers, in addition to all the other things asked of them, to be cultural trans-

24. *Le Figaro*, December 1, 1993

lators? I can't ask that of them if I don't give them the appropriate technical instruments. Neither will ideological speeches suffice, especially in an age when we are threatened with the death of ideology, death from uselessness.

The challenge must be embraced by those of us who are obliged to always carry forth the process of consciousness-raising, that is, by researchers. It is indispensable that we provide schools with didactic instruments for *working with diversity, not negating it or isolating it or simply tolerating it. But not viewing diversity as a necessary evil either, or celebrating it as a good in and of itself, without taking into account its dramatic side.*

To transform known and acknowledged diversity into a pedagogical advantage seems to me to be the great challenge for the future. We are learning to do it in the case of literacy, but it must be carried to its ultimate critical consequence: teaching literacy by turning differences in age within a single group, differences in dialect, differences in language and culture into pedagogical advantages. This is a necessity not only for countries in the South. The North too is discovering that monolingualism is a myth whose inevitable consequence is discrimination.

"Equivalence in difference is the cardinal problem of language," Jakobson said. *Equivalence is not levelling, but rather comparability.* Translation does not make equal: it simply allows for comparison. "Equivalence in difference" is probably the best way of characterizing the central issue in education for the immediate future, and very particularly the central issue in basic literacy.

Bibliography

Barbier Bouvet, Jean François, "Lire la page comme une image," in A. Bentolila (ed.), *Parole, Écrit, Image*, Les Entretiens Nathan, Actes III (Paris: Nathan, 1993), pp. 225-240.

Blanche-Benveniste, Claire, "Les unités: langue écrite, langue orale," in *Proceedings of the Workshop on Orality versus Literacy: Concepts, Methods and Data* (Strasbourg: European Science Foundation, 1993).

Bottéro, Jean, "L'écriture et la formation de l'intelligence en Mésopotamie ancienne," in *Le Débat*, No. 62, 1990, pp. 38-60. [Spanish edition: J. Bottéro et al, *Cultura, pensamiento, escritura* (Barcelona: Gedisa, Collección LeA, 1995).]

Brice-Heath, Shirley, *La política del lenguaje en México* (Mexico City: Instituto Nacional Indigenista, 1986).

Chartier, Roger, *Le livre en révolutions* (Paris: Éditions Textuel, 1997). [Spanish edition: R. Chartier, *Las revoluciones del libro* (Barcelona: Gedisa, Collección LeA, 2000).]

Cristal, David, *The Cambridge Encyclopedia of Language*

(Cambridge: Cambridge University Press, 1987, 6th edition, 1993).

Detienne, Marcel, *The Creation of Mythology* (Chicago: University of Chicago Press, 1986).

Ferreiro, Emilia, "Acerca de la necesaria coordinación entre semejanzas y diferencias," in J. A. Castorina, E. Ferreiro, M. Kohl and D. Lerner, *Piaget-Vigotsky: contribuciones para replantear el debate* (Buenos Aires: Paidós, 1996).

Godart, Louis, *L'invenzione della scrittura* (Torino: Einaudi, 1992).

Harris, William, *Ancient Literacy* (Cambridge and London: Harvard University Press, 1989).

Illich, Ivan, *Nella vigna del testo — Per una etologia della lettura* (Milan: Raffaello Cortina Editore, 1994). [English original: *In the Vineyard of the Text: A commentary to Hugh's Didascalion* (Chicago: University of Chicago Press, 1993). Spanish edition: *En el viñedo del texto. Un comentario al Didascalion de Hugo de San Víctor* (Mexico: Fondo de Cultura Económica).]

Jakobson, Roman, "On Linguistic Aspects of Translation," in *On Translation* (Cambridge: Harvard University Press, 1959).

Michalowski, Piotr, "Writing and Literacy in Early States: A Mesopotamianist Perspective," in D. Keller-Cohen (ed.), *Literacy: Interdisciplinary Conversations* (Cresskill, New Jersey: Hampton Press, 1994).

Ong, Walter, *Oralidad y escritura* (Mexico: Fondo de Cultura Económica, 1987). [English original, 1982.]

Parkes, Malcolm B., *Pause and Effect: An Introduction to the History of Punctuation in the West* (London: Scolar Press, 1992).

Pottier, Bernard, *América Latina en sus lenguas indígenas* (Caracas: UNESCO and Monte Ávila Editores, 1983).

Saenger, Paul, *Space Between Words: The Origins of Silent Reading* (Stanford, California: Stanford University Press, 1997).

"Lire aux derniers siècles du Moyen Age," in G. Cavallo and R. Chartier (eds.), *Histoire de la lecture dans le monde occidental* (Paris: Éditions du Seuil, 1997), pp. 147-174. [Spanish edition: *Historia de la lectura en el mundo occidental* (Madrid: Taurus, 1997).]

Sampson, Geoffrey, *Writing Systems* (London: Hutchinson, 1985). [Spanish edition: G. Sampson, *Sistemas de escritura — Análisis lingüístico* (Barcelona: Gedisa, Colección LeA).]

Samuels, Joe, "The state of education in South Africa," in B. Nasson and J. Samuels (eds.), *Education: From Poverty to Liberty* (Cape Town and Johannesburg: David Philip, 1990).

Thompson, Dorothy, "Conquest and Literacy: The Case of Ptolemaic Egypt," in D. Keller-Cohen (ed.), *Literacy: Interdisciplinary Conversations* (Cresskill, New Jersey: Hampton Press, 1994).